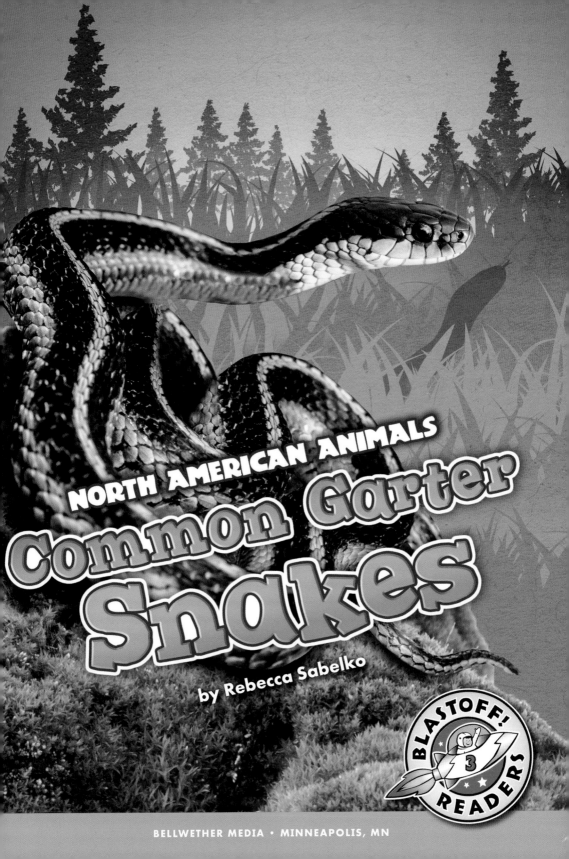

NORTH AMERICAN ANIMALS

Common Garter Snakes

by Rebecca Sabelko

BLASTOFF!
READERS
3

BELLWETHER MEDIA • MINNEAPOLIS, MN

Note to Librarians, Teachers, and Parents:

Blastoff! Readers are carefully developed by literacy experts and combine standards-based content with developmentally appropriate text.

Level 1 provides the most support through repetition of high-frequency words, light text, predictable sentence patterns, and strong visual support.

Level 2 offers early readers a bit more challenge through varied simple sentences, increased text load, and less repetition of high-frequency words.

Level 3 advances early-fluent readers toward fluency through increased text and concept load, less reliance on visuals, longer sentences, and more literary language.

Level 4 builds reading stamina by providing more text per page, increased use of punctuation, greater variation in sentence patterns, and increasingly challenging vocabulary.

Level 5 encourages children to move from "learning to read" to "reading to learn" by providing even more text, varied writing styles, and less familiar topics.

Whichever book is right for your reader, Blastoff! Readers are the perfect books to build confidence and encourage a love of reading that will last a lifetime!

This edition first published in 2019 by Bellwether Media, Inc.

No part of this publication may be reproduced in whole or in part without written permission of the publisher. For information regarding permission, write to Bellwether Media, Inc., Attention: Permissions Department, 6012 Blue Circle Drive, Minnetonka, MN 55343.

Library of Congress Cataloging-in-Publication Data

Names: Sabelko, Rebecca, author.
Title: Common Garter Snakes / by Rebecca Sabelko.
Description: Minneapolis, MN : Bellwether Media, Inc., 2019. | Series:
    Blastoff! Readers. North American Animals | Audience: Age 5-8. | Audience:
    K to Grade 3. | Includes bibliographical references and index.
Identifiers: LCCN 2018030420 (print) | LCCN 2018032388 (ebook) | ISBN
    9781681036410 (ebook) | ISBN 9781626179103 (hardcover : alk. paper)
Subjects: LCSH: Common garter snake–Juvenile literature.
Classification: LCC QL666.O636 (ebook) | LCC QL666.O636 S23 2019 (print) | DDC 597.96/2–dc23
LC record available at https://lccn.loc.gov/2018030420

Editor: Kate Moening   Designer: Josh Brink

Printed in the United States of America, North Mankato, MN.

Table of **Contents**

What Are Common Garter Snakes?

Common garter snakes are **reptiles** that live throughout much of the United States and southern Canada.

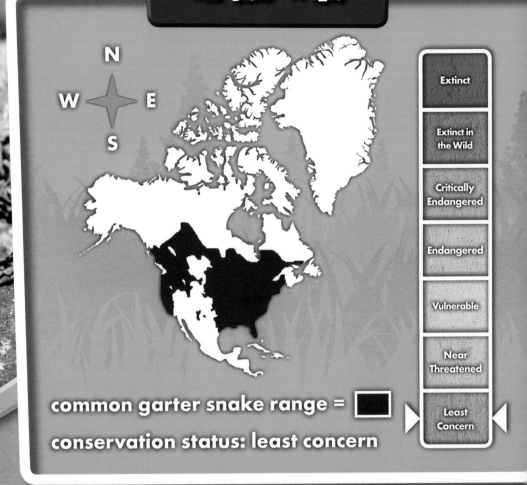

common garter snake range = ⬛

conservation status: least concern

Extinct

Extinct in the Wild

Critically Endangered

Endangered

Vulnerable

Near Threatened

Least Concern

These snakes do not like dry **climates**. But some live on mountain ranges in the Southwest U.S. and northern Mexico.

These reptiles make homes in **meadows** and woodlands. They often live close to water.

Common garter snakes hide from **predators** in tall grass. They also hide under rocks and logs.

Colors and Patterns

stripes

Most common garter snakes have three stripes. These are often white or yellow.

Identify a Common Garter Snake

black-tipped tongue

stripes

raised scales

Stripes help the snakes blend in with grass and other plants. Their dark-colored **scales** help them stay hidden, too.

9

Most common garter snakes are around 35 inches (90 centimeters) long. These **cold-blooded** animals warm their long bodies by taking in heat from the sun.

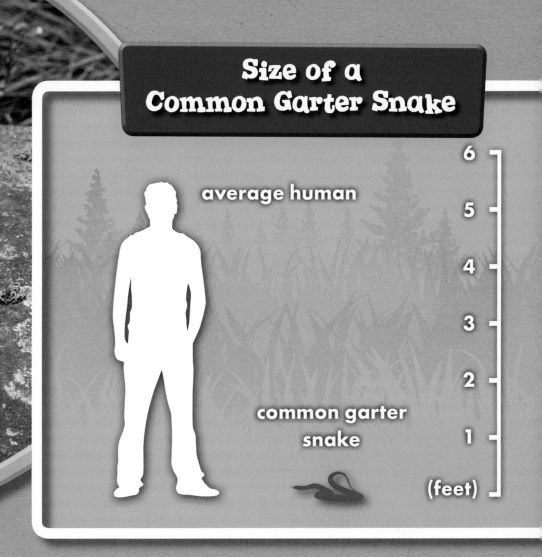

Size of a Common Garter Snake

average human

common garter snake

6

5

4

3

2

1

(feet)

During the winter, many **hibernate** in groups to stay warm. Thousands of common garter snakes may **coil** together in **dens**!

Common garter snakes poke their tongues in and out of their mouths while they hunt. This is how they smell their **prey**!

They can also sense **vibrations** in the ground. This lets them know if food is close.

On the Menu

northern leopard
frogs

common house
mice

leopard slugs

earthworms

American toads

mosquitofish

These **carnivores** are skilled
predators. They use quick
movements and sharp teeth
to catch prey.

14

Common garter snakes swallow small animals whole. They often need to chew larger prey.

Common garter snakes have many enemies. But their stripes and speed make these snakes hard to follow.

Animals to Avoid

American crows

raccoons

bullfrogs

domestic cats

great blue herons

red-tailed hawks

They give off a stinky smell when they are caught. This makes their predators think they taste bad!

Independent Babies

In late summer, female common garter snakes are ready to give birth to their young. Most females have 20 to 40 **snakelets**. But they may have up to 80!

Baby Facts

Name for babies:	snakelets
Size of litter:	up to 80 snakelets
Length of pregnancy:	2 to 3 months
Time spent with mom:	1 day

Snakelets are on their own
from the moment they are born.
But they may stay near their
mom for a few days.

Soon, these hungry babies are ready to hunt. They set off to find their first meal!

Glossary

carnivores—animals that only eat meat

climates—the specific long-term weather conditions for certain areas

coil—to form a series of loops

cold-blooded—having to get body heat from surroundings

dens—sheltered places

hibernate—to spend the winter sleeping or resting

meadows—fields of grass

predators—animals that hunt other animals for food

prey—animals that are hunted by other animals for food

reptiles—cold-blooded animals that have backbones and lay eggs

scales—small plates of skin that cover and protect a common garter snake's body

snakelets—baby common garter snakes

vibrations—very quick back-and-forth movements

To Learn More

AT THE LIBRARY
Gish, Melissa. *Snakes*. Mankato, Minn.: Creative
Education, 2018.

Gray, Susan H. *Snakes Shed Their Skin*. Ann Arbor,
Mich.: Cherry Lake Publishing, 2016.

Petrie, Kristin. *Garter Snakes*. Minneapolis, Minn.:
Checkerboard Library, 2015.

ON THE WEB

FACTSURFER

Factsurfer.com gives you
a safe, fun way to find
more information.

1. Go to www.factsurfer.com.

2. Enter "common garter snakes" into the search box.

3. Click the "Surf" button and select your
   book cover to see a list of related web sites.

Index

The images in this book are reproduced through the courtesy of: teekaygee, front cover (snake head), pp. 8-9; Jay Ondreicka, front cover (snake body), pp. 4-5, 9 (stripes, scales); valzan, front cover (log); CSP_secheltgirl/ agefotostock, p. 6; Zsombii, p. 7; Sharon Day, p. 9 (tongue); Michiel de Wi, pp. 9 (full snake), 14 (frogs, toads); Jason Ondreicka/ Alamy, pp. 10-11; Ron Rowan Photography, p. 12; FotoReques, p. 13; IrinaK, p. 14 (mice); Meister Photos, p. 14 (slugs); hsagencia, p. 14 (worms); gualtiero boffi, p. 14 (mosquitofish); Don Johnston/ Alamy, p. 15; Don Johnston, pp. 16-17; K Quinn Ferris, p. 17 (crows); Eric Isselee, p. 17 (raccoons); JIANG HONGYAN, p. 17 (bullfrogs); Chirtsova Natalia, p. 17 (cats); Tathoms, p. 17 (herons); Le Do, p. 17 (hawks); Zigmund Leszczynski/ agefotostock, pp. 18-19; Steve Byland, p. 19 (snake); By nasidastudio, p. 19 (rock); db_beyer, p. 20; BufferedBrain, p. 21.